CW00555049

Critical Thinking Unleashed

How To Improve And Refine Your Thinking Process To Think More Effectively

By

Christopher Hayes

Table of Contents

Introduction

Critical thinking is highly acclaimed as the best way to train your mind to think better. It is a way to improve your quality of thinking through rational and unbiased evaluation of factual evidence. People use critical thinking skills every day and they are extremely important in several situations such as the academic and work world.

There are many characteristics of a good critical thinker and plenty of processes and strategies you can use to become a better critical thinker. There are also certain things that completely derail critical thinking and lead to an unproductive, biased and closed-minded way of thinking contributes to many of the problems we face in the world today.

If more people used critical thinking skills as often as possible, it could lead to immense innovation, deep conversations and the elimination of a lot of the prejudices that are experienced everywhere.

Critical thinking is difficult to learn. Not everyone is born a natural critical thinker and to become a critical thinker requires long and consistent practice.

In that case, you might think, why should I even learn critical thinking? What if I'm not a natural-born critical thinker?

Fortunately, there are plenty of ways you can start practicing critical thinking skills no matter what age you are. If you use them as often as possible, before you know it; you will find yourself able to take in large quantities of information, quickly summarize important details, clearly communicate and justify your own arguments and more.

As a researcher who is always on the lookout for ways to improve the lifestyle and thought patterns of myself and others, and has put many of the strategies discussed in this book into practice, I am here to help you learn ways to improve your own critical thinking skills.

The world of critical thinking is vast and can be hard to know where to begin, but taking it one step at a time and going at your own pace, you will soon find yourself thinking clearer, solving problems in a more organized way and seeing the world in a different way.

Basics Of Critical Thinking

Critical thinking is something that people use every day, likely without even realizing they are actually doing it.

There may have been a time where a friend has needed support. Although they did not say it out loud, through interpreting their emotions and body language, you could tell that they needed help and could offer them advice. Perhaps there was a dispute at work and you found a way to compromise between opposing ideas. Or maybe you have budgeted your monthly paycheck to determine how much you will have to spend after necessities such as rent and food.

These are all examples of critical thinking. People use it every day to a certain extent and some use it more than others. However, developing critical thinking skills is essential to starting to live a better quality of life and opening your mind to new possibilities.

According to The Foundation For Critical Thinking, critical thinking is defined as a way of thinking where a person improves their quality of thinking by analyzing, assessing and reconstructing the particular subject at hand. These can be any subject, content or problem. [27]

It is self-directed, self-disciplined, self-monitored, and self-corrective thinking which involves effective communication and problem-solving abilities and a commitment to overcome our own egocentrism and sociocentrism, or preconceived notions about ourselves and the world we are familiar with.

Characterized by careful analysis and judgment, critical thinkers aim their thoughts at the well-founded judgment of a situation based on an appropriate evaluation of their surroundings determining its truth, worth or value before determining the outcome. [27]

Research into critical thinking shows that typically human thoughts are predisposed to prejudice, over-generalization, common fallacies, self-deception, rigidity, and narrowness. However, when critical thinking skills are applied, it is a way of training the mind to see past the usual errors in the way people think. It also proves that although people's mind tends to gravitate towards things like narrowness and prejudice without training, the mind can develop good reasoning abilities. [4]

Past research on critical thinking shows there are two intellectual tendencies that people usually fall into: [4]

- **The Majority**: One is the tendency of the majority to accept whatever most people believe to be true. In this way of thinking, people look at situations uncritically and feel that because things have been a certain way for a period of time and because most people feel that way, then it must be true and they do not take it upon themselves to come up with something different.

- **The Minority**: Another tendency is to question what is commonly accepted and to seek out answers for oneself. People who fall into this category actively utilize their critical thinking skills in their day-to-day life. They have established more reflective criteria for determining their own standards of judgment and do not take something as being true just because they are told so and the people around them believe it.

As you embark on your journey to becoming a better thinker, you will no doubt pass through the phases of critical thinking. There are six stages of development you can expect to pass through as you practice and cultivate your critical thinking skills over time. [32]

- **The Unreflective Thinker**: Assuming that you are starting at the very beginning when improving your critical thinking skills, the first stage you will go through is the unreflective thinker. Those in phase one are mainly unaware of the important role that critical thinking plays in their lives and also lack the ability to assess their thought patterns and improve them. Although it is possible for The Unreflective Thinker to have developed a variety of skills up to this point, they are unaware that they possess them.

- **The Challenged Thinker**: It is this phase where you realize the important role that critical thinking plays in your life. They realize that high-quality thinking comes through reflective thinking and they recognize that most thinking is flawed. Although they have limited critical thinking skills, they might feel that the skills they have unconsciously developed make them better thinkers than they are, and they have to accept the challenge to improve.

- **The Beginning Thinker**: In the third phase, you have accepted the challenge to become a better thinker and are already taking steps to improve. At this stage, people realize the basic problem in their thinking and are taking steps to correct them. At this phase, you also realize the key concepts of critical thinking such as concepts, assumptions, inferences, implications, and points of view. Additionally, beginner thinkers can appreciate criticism of their current thought processes because it allows them to see how they can improve.

- **The Practicing Thinker**: At this phase, people have a sense of the habits they need to develop to become full-fledged critical thinkers. They also understand the need to fix their thinking in a systematic way and can actively analyze their thinking in different domains. At this phase, you will have enough skills to monitor your thoughts regularly and correct them on the spot. You can also recognize your own egocentricities, the role they play in your critical thinking, and how to correct them.

- **The Advanced Thinker**: At this point, the good habits of thought you have established are starting to pay off. You are actively analyzing your thinking in all of the specific domains of your life and have insight into problems on a deeper level. Advanced thinkers are very knowledgeable of what it takes to regularly assess their own thinking for clarity and precision. So, they are always on the road to improvement.

- **The Accomplished Thinker**: Being at the final stage does not mean you would have mastered critical thinking completely because critical thinking is always an ongoing learning process. However, at this stage, you will have deeply internalized the basic skills of thought so your critical thinking is conscious and highly intuitive.

In addition to improving your quality of thinking, critical thinking serves to help you organize your thoughts. Instead of letting emotions get in the way of your thinking, it allows you to take a step back, regroup, and approach your thoughts from a more objective standpoint. With this self-guided and self-disciplined type of thinking attempts to help you to reason at the highest level of quality in a fair-minded way.

Utilizing critical thinking skills make a positive impact on your quality of life as people who think critically tend to live rationally, reasonably, and empathically. This is because they do not let emotions and subjectivity get in the way of seeing things for what they truly are. They know of the flawed nature of human thinking when it is left unchecked and strive to not let their own ego or their social environment get in the way. [4]

Further, critical thinking involves thinking outside of the box. However, if you want to think outside of the box, you need to establish creativity within your mind. [20]

Critical thinking and creativity go hand in hand. While critical thinking involves thinking clearly and rationally, following the rules of logic and scientific reasoning, creativity involves coming up with new and useful ideas as well as alternative possibilities. Creativity is necessary to solve problems; however, critical thinking is essential when it comes to evaluating and improving these ideas. Both are necessary and both are needed for people to ultimately prosper. [20]

Although creativity tends to be a little more spontaneous than critical thinking, it is similar to critical thinking in how it follows a step-by-step process. It is likely you have done something similar to this before without even realizing it. The Creativity Cycle involves four steps: [20]

- **Preparation**: This step is just like it sounds; you are setting up the framework for whatever it is you are trying to come up with. That means gathering information. You can read up on it in the library or online. You can also talk to other people to find out more. At this stage, you are collecting everything that might be relevant to the situation without very much filtering or analysis which comes in the next step.

> Imagine an artist who is putting together their next big work of art with the theme of the environment. They certainly can pull out their canvas and just make things up as they go along, but they want this creative masterpiece to be a thoughtful one. So, they pull together as many resources as they can find to make this as in-depth of a piece as they can possibly make it.

- **Exploration**: At this stage, you have collected all the information you need. Now it is time to look at what you have. This can include classifying your material, organizing it and looking at it from different perspectives. While devoting your attention to what you have found you might find there are things that might not be as useful to you as you thought, or you might find gaps that you need to fill.

Think of the artist who at this stage will have gathered everything they can have to do with the environment such as physical materials as well as written research. At this phase, the creative person will inspect everything to determine what they can and cannot use for their project as well as starting to piece together what the final project will be like.

- **Incubation**: Sometimes it is difficult to come up with a final plan and at that point it's a good idea to pause and let the idea sit with you for a while. Set the task aside for a moment, relax and come to it later. Chances are an idea will come to you when you are listening to music or taking a walk. The incubation stage lets you come back to the project later with a fresh eye and new ideas.

- **Verification**: Once you've come back to your project, it is time to see if it can work. This means putting everything together and seeing what the outcome will be. If the project was unsuccessful and didn't turn out the outcome you wanted, then it's time to go back to the drawing board. If it was successful, then look back on what went well so you can repeat the process.

The Creativity Cycle is a lot more common than you might think. How many items, projects or programs can you think of that may have followed this same process? Maybe at their verification phase, they found that their project wasn't as viable as they thought and had to start from the beginning or maybe it ended up being very successful and well known on the first try.

Although creativity is a little different from critical

thinking, the two are like brother and sister. True creativity uses critical thinking skills and creativity enhances critical thinking. While you will find the steps in The Creativity Cycle differ from the steps in critical thinking, you will also find they have some similarities. [20]

What Is Opposite To Critical Thinking?

Critical thinking is an active way of thinking where a person develops a set of skills to conceptualize, apply, analyze, and evaluate the information given to them. This is done through a variety of methods such as observation, experience, reflection, or communication. It develops one's beliefs and actions to organize thoughts to form opinions from an objective standpoint and are essential to creative thought.

Those who are not using their critical thinking skills fall into the habit of passive thinking.

Passive thinkers operate under the mindset that things are happening to them instead of making things happen themselves and they are not responsible for the things that happen to them. Instead, they fall into the "pack" mentality, meaning they go along with what others think instead of using the analytical skills of a critical thinker to discover answers for themselves. [25]

If someone says something is true, the passive thinker will believe it is so. If the people around them have a certain mindset, the passive thinker will not take it upon themselves to find a different perspective.

The quality of life of someone who continuously uses passive thinking reflects their mindset. Eventually, they will end up believing that nothing is their responsibility. Additionally, they go through life making passive associations. They allow whatever thoughts float through their mind to be at the forefront of their beliefs. Instead of the clarity and awareness that comes with critical thinking, they live blurrily. Their thoughts and beliefs are not set in stone and they are easily swayed. [25]

Part of passive thinking is gut thinking. This involves making decisions based on instinct instead of putting thought into what you are doing. It is made up of intuitive thinking, which is a feeling or sense that does not use rational processes to come to any conclusion. Think of it as having your brain on autopilot and you are just casually going along with it. [18]

There are cases when gut thinking comes in handy. Have you ever been in a situation where something just does not seem right? An everyday example might include being offered a great deal on something you are trying to buy but it seems too good to be true. You can't exactly pinpoint why, but intuition will tell you that it does not seem like a good idea. Sure enough, you turn it down and find out later that it was a scam.

We develop good intuition through practice. It comes from years of experience that allows you to discover just how the world and the people in it work. However, you should not rely on intuition for every decision you make. [25]

In situations that require a major decision, whether in your personal life, at work or any situation that affects others, it is often best to weigh the pros and cons of that decision, think it through and analyze it carefully before coming to any conclusion on it.

I can consider passive thinking a cause of many of the world's problems, such as racism, xenophobia and religious extremism. All of those ideologies have one thing in common: they result from closed-mindedness and an absence of true critical thinking as they fall into the trap of passive thinking.

A racist person is more likely the result of their

environment. Someone with this mindset may have spent much of their time surrounded by people open about their racist ideologies. Because they have used none critical thinking skills into the matter, they do not question the wrongful way of thinking it pushed onto them. Other people believe it, so it must be correct. They do not take the initiative to discover for themselves other perspectives, instead, remain set in the way of other people's mindset not bothering to find their own.

If they were to use critical thinking skills into the matter, they would question for themselves whether what they are being told is correct. They would take the initiative to do their own research on other ethnicities and cultures to understand them. They would find articles and news stories of ideologies opposite of their own to learn how others think. They might also go out and find people different from them to get to know them.

After putting into practice a set of critical thinking actions, they can form their own opinion of other races instead of following the majority they had been surrounded by.

On a day-to-day basis, lack of critical thinking can make everyday interactions much less meaningful than they could be. There are a few reasons society could be at fault for this. [4]

One would be how people are raised. From an early age, we teach people that having unconventional ideas is wrong. People are taught to be embarrassed about having a different view than others and are taught it is wrong to question the status quo. It conditions them on what is right, what is wrong, what is normal, and what is abnormal; and the moment they think about falling out of line with those preconceived set of standards, they feel that they are doing something wrong. [4]

Another could be the consumption of popular culture. With the omniscience of the internet, it is easy for people, especially young people, to be conditioned by what they see. Whether it is television or social media, the constant barrage of things has the possibility to make their imagination insular. They take what they see as a standard of how they should think and act and do not question it.

Benefits Of Critical Thinking Over Passive And Gut Thinking

Overall, critical thinking leads us to unlock our intellectual independence. It helps to move us away from rushed conclusions, mystification, and reluctance to question received wisdom, tradition, and authority. Unlike passive thinking, it moves us towards intellectual discipline, a clear expression of ideas and acceptance of personal responsibility for our own thinking.

There are quite a few benefits of critical thinking,

according to the Foundation for Critical Thinking: [6]

- Critical thinkers can raise vital questions when it comes to solving problems. They can form their questions clearly and precisely.
- Critical thinkers can gather and assess information related to a particular topic. Even better, they can use abstract ideas to interpret the topic more effectively.
- Critical thinkers can come to well-reasoned conclusions as well as test them among relevant criteria and standards.
- Critical thinkers are open-minded when it comes to alternative systems of thought. They can recognize and assess their assumptions, implications, and practical consequences of them.
- Critical thinkers can communicate effectively with others, able to figure out solutions to complex problems.

In many cases, non-intuitive thinking, or critical thinking, is the best way to make decisions over intuitive thinking.

This is especially true when there is no obvious solution to a problem. The passive or intuitive thinker might go with the first answer that pops into their mind but it might not end up being the correct answer.

Instead of just going with the first thing that enters your mind or going along with whatever someone else told you, critical thinking allows you to ask certain questions before you make a definitive conclusion: [25]

- Does this make sense?
- Why does it make sense? Or why not?
- How can I apply it?

Unlike passive thinking, critical thinking allows you to keep an open mind to new information as well as test new experiences and information against past experiences and information. Upon testing the information given to you, you will have a well-rounded frame of reference to either keep the opinion you held at first or form a new opinion.

During passive thinking, your mind is just going through the motions accepting what comes your way putting no intellectual thought forward to challenge it. There are several ways to grasp critical thinking ideas that not only provide insight during the present moment but enrich your life and strengthen your cognitive processes. [6]

- **Gaining Experience**: Experience is the world's best teacher. By gaining experience in as many areas as possible, you expand your knowledge base on a variety of topics and are better able to make connections when most needed. Experience teaches you what problems or objectives are straightforward and what is not, what to look for in several situations and what issues are the most important for you to address.

This can apply to any life experience whether it is gaining experience in your field of work, as a new parent, someone just beginning their college education and more. No matter where you find yourself, the experience will be essential in the long run to thinking critically about the positions you find yourself in.

- **Experimentation**: This can help you discover inconsistencies in a situation or train of thought. One way you can do this is by tinkering or doing a series of problem-solving activities that will enable you to learn by trial and error. This is a powerful critical thinking skill born out of curiosity and developed through discovery. In some cases, experimenting can be a leisurely activity, something done just for fun with no goals, deadlines or pressure but serves to let you learn at your own pace. Other times it can lead to a significant discovery that can be useful to you.

One example of experimentation is working on some mechanical object, like a car. If you have an interest in cars, or even if you don't, and you take the time to poke around seeing how things work this could yield several results. For one thing, you could learn something you didn't know before which could be useful to you the next time your car breaks down. Another benefit may be that you become equipped with the information you can use to critically assess a situation such as someone trying to sell you something you don't particularly need for the car or any other situation where you need to make a decision on the car.

- **Learning**: They say learning does not end once school is over. The more you grow your knowledge base, the more you know about all the little nuances and subtleties of life. The more you read, research, learn from others and partake in any other method to expand your knowledge of various topics, the more of a capacity you will have for critical thinking.

Critical thinking takes practice, and no one will use critical thinking every second of every day. The mind has a tendency to wander so everyone will have a tendency towards irrational or passive thought every now and then.

However, as a self-directed and self-disciplined mode of thought, critical thinking yields results and benefits when used correctly. This is where creativity comes into play. Thinking critically is the basis for coming up with new and innovative solutions to problems we face every day.

Used in a group, critical thinking can be even more useful not only to individuals but the world. The more people gathered from various and diverse disciplines, assembling together to solve our many problems, the better our society will be prepared for the future.

An everyday example involves a school. Several teachers have noticed they have students in their class who are falling behind in mathematics. One teacher brings it up to their colleague who shares their struggle and they think about how to fix the problem.

At their next planning meeting among the rest of the teachers in their department, they share their observations and other teachers express that they have noticed the same thing. Everyone has a shared problem, now the question remains of what to do about it.

So, they start brainstorming. They collectively come up with ideas that range from individual tutoring to having their students stay after class. After weighing all of their ideas, school resources and the time that would need to be given to help, they conclude that an after-school math tutoring program would be the best way to solve the problem. They then work together to arrange how the program will work.

On a larger scale, take, for example, a big county where people in different areas of the county have different needs. The needs of the northern half of the county differ vastly from those of the southern half and both sides feel like their concerns are not being heard by the county government.

The leaders of the county recognize this after complaints from throughout the area and come together to work towards a solution. The main question among them is what is the best way to address every part of the county and come up with objective and implementable solutions.

The group recognizes that town hall meetings have been successful in the past at drawing a substantial group of people. They hold individual meetings in various cities and towns throughout the county to get a hyper-local view of what people need, compile written feedback and then bring everyone together to review plans that can be implemented for the next year.

Premises And Arguments

Critical thinking is a rational thought pattern. It involves analyzing the problem at hand, thinking it through thoroughly allowing you to avoid rushed conclusions and planning a well-developed argument before drawing any conclusions. These characteristics are essential to organizing your thoughts in order to develop good premises and arguments.

At its core, a premise is a proposition that we base an argument on. From an argument, you can then draw conclusions. We can also think premises of as the reasons and evidence behind a conclusion. [9]

In a deductive argument, a premise can be a major or minor proposition of the argument in which we draw two conclusions from, also known as a syllogism, to draw logical conclusions. For example, "All mammals are warm-blooded," would be considered a major premise, "Whales are mammals," is the minor premise. Therefore, the conclusion to this argument would be, “Whales are warm-blooded.”

Premises are common in philosophy and in writing. In philosophy, arguments are more concerned with a set of premises that support a conclusion more so than disputes among people. [24]

Also, in philosophical arguments, we consider an argument valid if it follows logically through its premises, but the conclusion can still be invalid. The process of drawing a conclusion then involves a process of deductive reasoning.

You can say that “men are tall,” followed by, “the singer Prince is a man,” and conclude that “Prince is tall,” but this would be an inaccurate conclusion considering that Prince was known for being short at only five feet two inches tall.

In writing, particularly nonfiction writing, premises

typically follow the same rules as philosophical premises. The Purdue University Online Writing Lab (OWL) defines premises as an assertion of a conclusion based on logical premises and calls the syllogisms used in philosophy the simplest sequence of logical premises and conclusions. [24]

The difference between premises in philosophy and writing is that nonfiction writing, in general, rarely distinguishes between major and minor premises.

In nonfiction writing, it is common to see premises used as the basis of an editorial or an opinion piece or a letter to the editor. So, for example, your first premise might be, "Nonrenewable resources do not exist in infinite supply," and the second premise would be, "Coal is a nonrenewable resource." So, your conclusion is, "Coal does not exist in infinite supply." Not necessarily a major and minor premise, such as in philosophy, but the same rules still apply.

In fiction writing, the premise serves as the foundation for your story but does not necessarily try to form an argument like philosophical and nonfiction premises do. The characters the plot then prove or disprove the argument. [24]

If we take the story, "The Three Little Pigs," the premise there is that "Foolishness leads to death and wisdom leads to happiness." The argument itself does not prove its point through major and minor premises, but the characters and the plot of the story made the argument and prove it to be true by the end.

We can use premises in a variety of other arguments. Not limited to just philosophy and writing, we can use premises in science, theology and more.

Are There Good And Bad Arguments?

Anyone can come up with a premise for an argument. However, that does not necessarily mean your argument is a good argument. This is where your critical thinking skills come into play. It takes a little organization, problem-solving, and analyzing to come up with a good argument that makes sense and effectively supports the case you are trying to make.

The truthfulness or falsity of your argument does not so much have anything to do with ethics or morals as much as it is your reasons for giving the argument accurately. The reasons for the argument must be closely associated with the truth, meaning your premises must be correct to come up with a truthful argument. Good reason makes belief more probable, and vice versa. The very best reasons make it certain. [12]

There are a few characteristics essential to a good, or

truthful, argument. [12]

- **Valid**: If your argument is invalid, it will ultimately lead to a bad argument. It would be intended to give conclusive support for its conclusion instead of building up to the conclusion through an argument that makes sense.

- **Strong**: A strong argument is difficult to dispute. In a weak argument, many other viable conclusions can be formed from the argument and then your conclusion ends up falling apart. Strong arguments are the kinds of arguments you want to strive for.

- **Sound**: A sound argument involves premises that are true. This is essential in planning a good argument. If your premises are not true, your argument falls apart, and your conclusion ends up being false.

- **Cogent**: This means your argument is clear, logical and convincing. Think of your argument being cogent as the end goal of your argument: if your premises are false and your argument is invalid and weak, then your argument is not cogent and therefore a bad argument.

Where good arguments have their reasons based on truth, bad arguments have their reasons based in falsehood. These arguments are misleading, whether or not intentional, and dismantle what could be a valid, strong, sound, and cogent argument.

Like truthful arguments, there are also a few characteristics that go along with false arguments. [13]

- **Dubious Premises**: Arguments that depend on dubious premises are inherently false arguments because they are suspicious, untrustworthy, unreliable, and questionable. They depend on the hope that the audience will misunderstand or completely fail to understand the argument. They can also benefit from a particular context such as an advertisement that would say a product is a high quality although it is not.

A dubious premise can mislead by assuming the answer to a question before it even comes up, such as, "Have you stopped cheating?" Additionally, dubious premises may lead to arguments which contain premises that are insufficiently informative or complete nonsense.

- **Fallacies**: A fallacy often arises from vagueness, ambiguity, and equivocation in the premise which makes it impossible for the audience to accept them as true. Fallacies can also occur when the conclusion of the argument either supports the premise or merely restates the premise. These fall apart because they end up not being derived from the argument itself.

Fallacies can be even further weakened by irrelevance, meaning that the argument brings in irrelevant information intending to divert the audience's attention away from the argument itself.

There are a few different types of fallacies that intend to divert attention away from the argument. The most common are ad hominem fallacies that are directed at the opinion holder in the argument. We can consider these abusive attacks or circumstantial. Tu quoque fallacies accuse the opinion holder of inconsistency or hypocrisy. They fail to address the opinion holder's argument itself. Straw man fallacies set up inaccurate reconstructions of someone's argument in an attempt to criticize it. Finally, ad populum fallacies try to convince the audience that the argument is correct because it is popular.

- **Hasty Conclusions**: Arguments with hasty conclusions tend to employ what is called enthymematic premises. These are premises that are intentionally suppressed, accidentally overlooked and are dubious. These hasty conclusions also employ other types of fallacies and diversions to draw their conclusion faster. Another way arguments can draw hasty conclusions is by appealing to ignorance to support a conclusion as they suggest that if something has not been shown to be true, then it must be false.

How Premises Lead To A Conclusion, And How To Analyze Premises?

Premises are essential to composing a truthful argument. What follows the argument is the conclusion. There are specific ways to get there from the formulation of your premise.

We can consider premises and conclusions the basic building blocks of an argument. We know that premises are assertions or pieces of evidence that lead to a conclusion but the trouble is how we get to the conclusion in the first place.

First, let's look at the conclusions. We can look a conclusion as an assertion that your audience will not readily accept. For example, your conclusion can be, "The lake is deep." The person you are presenting this conclusion to can easily follow up with, "Well, what evidence do you have that this lake is deep?" [14]

All conclusions need to have at least one premise that supports it. Think of it as a paper written for a class. They start out with a thesis, followed by several paragraphs that contain your main points and they always end with a conclusion that is supported by the preceding argument.

So, taking the above example, if you change your argument to add the premise that, "All lakes in this region are deep," you can conclude that this lake is deep.

Sometimes differentiating between premises and conclusions can be confusing. To make things easier, look for indicator words that signal which part of the argument is the premise and which is the conclusion. Also known as joining words, these act as a transition between the premise and conclusion. [14]

Indicator words that are included with premises include words such as because, but, since, given that, and or considering that. For conclusions, indicator words include, therefore, thus, which follows that consequently and so.

These are useful to know if you have an argument where the conclusion comes before the premise. For example, in the argument, "You need to drink water because your body cannot survive without water," you can tell the premise follows the conclusion by the indicator word, "because."

There is a process you can follow for analyzing a

premise. This is a way of evaluating the information given to us in a disciplined way.

- **Analyzing**: This is an important first step because it involves examining the argument methodically and in detail to get to know the structure of the argument. This includes breaking down what parts of the arguments are premises and which parts are conclusions, that way you can then find out what the purpose of the argument is.

  So if we analyze the argument, "Poodles are small dogs and I have heard that they do not shed, so you should get a poodle," we can determine that "poodles are small dogs," and, "I have heard that they do not shed," are the premises and, "you should get a poodle," is the conclusion.

- **Conceptualizing**: This means forming an idea about something. When you conceptualize, it helps to produce an image in your mind or come up with an analogy that you can relate to much easier. In the case of the poodle, you might imagine what a poodle looks like; a small, fluffy dog. You can also imagine the dog in comparison to your home. How small would you want your dog to be? How tall is it compared to your furniture? Can you imagine how easy or difficult it would be to clean up after a dog if it shed a lot?

- **Defining**: Defining something involves stating or describing the exact nature, scope or meaning of something. In the case of your argument, at this step, you would try to explain, interpret and clarify it. Here, break down each premise and interpret exactly what it means. "Poodles are small dogs." What would you consider to be a small dog? Maybe something between one and two feet tall. "I have heard that they do not shed?" You know that shedding involves a dog losing a lot of hair throughout the day that the owner has to clean up from furniture, carpets, and clothing.

- **Examining**: Investigating involves inspecting something thoroughly. Here you want to determine the nature or condition of your argument, while even testing the knowledge of it. This is where you ask yourself some additional questions about the premise. Is there any way that you can dispute this? Are there any alternative arguments to it?

- **Inferring**: At this step, you ask yourself if there is anything you can deduce or conclude from the premise. Naturally, this might be the conclusion that "you should get a poodle," but ask yourself if there are any alternative conclusions that you can infer from the premise. If not, you can consider this a deductive argument.

- **Listening**: This is important in any situation and here it will be key to ensuring that you have heard every aspect of the argument so you have everything you need to draw your conclusion from it and determine that it is, in fact, a truthful argument.

- **Questioning**: We know that a deductive argument leaves no room for you to question its conclusion. At this step, go over each premise again and see if you can point out questions about the conclusion that might prove it to be false.

- **Reasoning**: This is the act of thinking about something in a logical and sensible way. Does each premise make sense? We know that poodles are considered small dogs as well as the fact that they don't shed. Based on the circumstances of these premises, does the conclusion that you should get a poodle also seem logical?

- **Synthesizing**: This is the stage where you put it all together. You have thoroughly examined each premise and asked all the questions that you can. If there are no further questions or alternatives, it is safe to say that what you have is a truthful argument. The conclusion, "You should get a poodle," meets criteria of being a valid, sound, strong, cogent, and deductive argument.

Deductive And Ampliative Arguments

Another sign of a good argument is if it is deductive. One way to determine if an argument is substantial or not is to determine how well the premises of the argument supports its conclusion. The more they support the argument, the more deductive the argument is.

We can describe deductive arguments as arguments to guarantee that the truth of the conclusion as long as the premises of the argument are true. This means the argument is deductively valid. [9]

In these types of arguments, the premises must provide such strong support for the conclusion that if the premises are true, then it would be impossible to determine that the conclusion is false, thus a stronger argument. As long as the premises guarantee the conclusion is true, this is considered a valid argument. Valid arguments have true premises, are considered sound. [9]

To look at an example of a deductive argument: “It is sunny in the city. If it is sunny in the city, Joe will not take an umbrella with him. Therefore, he will not carry an umbrella.”

Both the premises of the argument support the conclusion so it makes sense to conclude that Joe will not take an umbrella with him because it is sunny in the city. The argument is sound, and it is also valid because the premises guarantee that the conclusion is true, and they give no room for evidence that would say otherwise.

The opposite of deductive arguments is inductive, or

an ampliative reasoning. While deductive arguments find their conclusion based on the premises provided in the argument, ampliative arguments interpret the evidence based on the conclusion. It amplifies the evidence through methods of generalizing, predicting or uncovering the best account of this evidence. [9]

Ampliative arguments attempt to prove that their argument is strong enough that if this argument were to be true, then it would be unlikely that the conclusion is false. Ampliative arguments are not as definitive as deductive arguments as it bases their strength on the degree to which we consider their argument likely to be true.

To take an example of an ampliative argument: "Today Ashley said she is tired, so Ashley told her mom she is tired."

This conclusion of this ampliative argument is not as definite as it would be if it were a deductive argument.

It leaves a lot of room to dispute the conclusion. You could ask why Ashley is tired or does Ashley show any evidence of being tired.

Ampliative arguments can be made into more deductive arguments with the addition of a premise. This provides evidence to support the argument. Think of the difference between deductive and ampliative arguments as a threshold: ampliative arguments leave room to add more premises, or evidence, to support their conclusion while deductive arguments do not.

So, if you were to add another premise to this ampliative argument it becomes stronger.

"Ashley worked a long shift today. Ashley is tired. So, Ashley told her mom she is tired because she worked a long shift."

The ampliative argument becomes more valid with the addition of the premise that justifies the conclusion of Ashley telling her mom she is tired.

A lot of times, people use ampliative arguments as if they were deductive.

Keep in mind the key differences between deductive and ampliative arguments. It is easy to get them confused because the only thing separating an ampliative argument from a deductive argument is the addition of a premise that makes the argument more specific. [15]

We can think deductive arguments of as arguing from a general idea to a specific one while ampliative arguments would argue from a specific idea to a general one. The two are related, however, it is only one key phrase that separates them. [15]

Deductive arguments attempt to provide grounds for making their conclusion and if they succeed, we consider the argument valid. Most importantly, the premises of the argument must be true. If both things are the case, then you can consider it a sound and truthful argument.

Although just as common as deductive arguments, ampliative arguments attempt to provide the grounds for the argument to be likely or probable.

Main Features Of A Critical Thinker

Most people have to know someone in their life who consistently puts into practice critical thinking skills. This is probably the person who is very knowledgeable about certain topics, forms their own opinion about things, always coming up with solutions to problems, and usually knows the best way of going about solving these problems.

Have you ever thought about what really sets them apart as a critical thinker though? Are there any characteristics they seem to display in everyday situations that distinguish them as someone who uses critical thinking skills daily?

To illustrate the different characteristics of certain people, think of two people faced with a situation. These people would be considered the critical thinker and the passive thinker.

Both people work in a retail store and face a situation where a customer wants to return an item. Returns at this store are tricky and they are not sure of how to do it on their own. The differences in their thought patterns determine how each person will respond to this situation.

The passive thinker is not one to be creative. They were shown how to do a return during their training at the store, but again, returns are tricky, and they don't remember all the steps.

They do not take the time to assess the situation and look for the resources at their disposal that will help them perform the return. Instead of examining the situation thoroughly, they don't put forth the effort to find a solution to the problem.

The passive thinker takes up the mentality that they don't know what to do so it cannot be done. They may feel defeated or they may even convince themselves that it does not matter. They tell the customer, "Sorry, I don't know how to do that. Come another time," and leave the situation as it is.

However, the critical thinker takes a different approach. Curious and resourceful, the critical thinker immediately takes it upon themselves to find a solution. With an open-minded perspective and the ability to handle uncertainty, they walk through all the steps of critical thinking as they try to find an answer.

They run through all of their options: clicking around in the computer system to figure it out, looking through the instruction manuals that the store provides, calls customer service and the store manager. Finally, after exhausting all of their options and analyzing the situation as thoroughly as possible, they find an answer to the problem.

There are certain characteristics that distinguish a critical thinker from a passive thinker. This involves everything from how they view the world, their approach to a problem and the steps they take to find answers.

The passive thinker gives up easily, has a narrow perspective, and does not take the initiative to discover answers that aren't very clear to them.

However, there are a few different characteristics that set critical thinkers apart from others.

- **Curiosity**: You could say this is the first step towards becoming a critical thinker. People who are good critical thinkers have to be curious about the situations they find themselves in and just life. This is how the critical thinker asks the questions that set them off to discover new perspectives and ideas. They ask the who, what, when, where, why, and how questions that allow for fully informed, well-rounded answers, and even innovation.

To take the retail situation, for example, the

difference in how the critical thinker and the passive thinker approached the situation began with curiosity. The passive thinker did not bother to ask themselves questions about the situation. On the other hand, the critical thinker asked how I can do this. They wanted to gain a new skill and were curious about how to achieve what had been so difficult for them in the past.

- **A Wide Perspective**: This is another characteristic essential to being a critical thinker. If someone is narrow-minded and not open to new possibilities, then they will not find themselves able to accept new ideas, new strategies and be able to accept new possibilities. A wide perspective enables the critical thinker to step outside their own box and find out what lies ahead of them.

In the retail example, the critical thinker could use the resources at their disposals such as the guidebook the store provided to them and the customer service line because they were open-minded about the possibilities of how to perform this return and help the customer. Whereas a passive thinker's mind did not get to the idea of using any resources. With the narrow-minded thinking of "I don't know what to do so I can't do this," is a negative premise, a closed perspective and did not leave them with the open-mindedness necessary to solve the problem at hand.

- **Broad Knowledge**: What you may have noticed about the critical thinkers in your life is that they have a vast knowledge of a variety of topics. Often critical thinkers read books, consuming news about current events and going out to experience things firsthand, like going to a museum.

  Learning is such an essential step to strengthening your critical thinking skills because the more you know about a range of topics, the more often you will think critically about any situation or topic that presents itself to you. If someone is very knowledgeable about the history, they will notice patterns in current events that mirror past events and infer what happened at a previous point in time. Or if someone possesses a lot of knowledge in politics, they have more of an advantage when it comes to the ability to think critically about political events such as presidential debates.

- **Being Properly Informed About the Subject**: When it comes to thinking critically, while a lot of knowledge is important, it is even more important to have accurate knowledge. A person can learn as much as they want, but if they are not properly informed about a subject, then their knowledge is useless.

Take the history buff again. A person can be extremely interested in history and have consumed several books about various historical periods. But if their knowledge of a subject is completely misinformed, for example, Ancient Rome, then their argument that present-day America is mirroring the fall of Rome becomes inaccurate.

- **Examining the Reasoning and Possible Biases and The Assumptions Behind Them**: Not only can critical thinkers formulate accurate and sound reasoning behind an argument, but they also possess the ability to recognize any kind of bias among that reasoning whether it is their own or the biases of someone else. If a political argument is brought to them, they can recognize the bias that comes with party affiliation and separates that from the situation to create a sound argument. Or if a new teacher comes into their school and they are wonderful, the critical thinker can put aside their own biases and objectively explain why this teacher is so great.

- **The Possession of Reasoning Based on Sound Consistent Logic**: If the logic behind the reasoning of an argument is inconsistent, then ultimately, the entire argument falls apart. If the premises of an argument are, “Water is wet, rain is water,” but they conclude with, “The rain is not wet,” there is no logic behind that argument. Not only does the critical thinker possess this reasoning, but they do it with no emotions or social pressure behind it. Their own emotions or the pressure they experience from their peers only served to make their argument biased which they try to avoid in the first place.

- **Ability to Handle Uncertainty**: This is very important in situations where critical thinking is necessary. Sometimes there is a problem that needs to be solved and the answers are not obvious. The critical thinker does not fall apart and give up when uncertainty arises. Like the retail worker, the critical thinker possesses the ability to remain calm in uncertain situations. They can determine exactly what needs to be done, all the while staying level-headed.

- **Aware of Their Own Areas of Ignorance**: Besides being aware of their own biases, the critical thinker is also aware of their own ignorance in a situation. It's not possible for someone to know everything so when the critical thinker encounters something they are unsure of; they recognize it and try to find the answers. On top of this, they do not make up information to fill in what they do not know.

- **They Can Wait for Valid Evidence and Evidence-Based Answers**: Evidence is essential to forming a valid and sound argument. You cannot draw a good conclusion from an argument without sound evidence. Critical thinkers recognize how important evidence is to an argument and will find sufficient evidence to support their argument no matter what.

Things That Sabotage Critical Thinking

Overall, there are too many reasons people do not think critically. One of them is that people have become so busy (or lazy) they allow other people to think for them. Another is that it is so easy to distort the truth through what we call perception.

The critical thinker, however, challenges environmental myths, distortions of the truth, political special interests, Gladwell, corporate bureaucracy, groupthink, and anything that goes against good, old-fashioned investigative thinking and critical thinking. [17]

Certainly, anyone can learn to think more critically if they put their mind to it and commit to practicing it daily. However, most people do not think critically as much as they think they do. One thing that really sabotages critical thinking in anyone is that most people try to avoid thinking.

Thinking critically takes a lot of effort, much more effort than most people want to put in on a day-to-day basis. There are a few techniques that people employ so they don't have to think critically as much as they should. [17]

The first is the "monkey mind," what Buddhists used to describe mental distraction. With this technique, the mind wanders and jumps from thought to thought with no direction. Picture it like a monkey jumping back and forth from tree to tree trying to let out its frustrations.

Another technique is the "gator brain". This is the primitive part of the mind where its main objective is survival. When threatened the mind reverts to its primitive actions such as eating or the fight-or-flight response. This is fine in a dangerous situation, however, daily, this only leads to dysfunction.

Finally, there is just allowing yourself to become comfortable in one state of mind. If you become comfortable thinking one way, you won't push yourself to think differently or do anything out of the ordinary. Even worse, you will feel you cannot think differently in the first place, so you will not try. If you can't break these patterns when necessary, you become trapped in this reduced mindset.

Apart from just not thinking, there are a few different ways people can intentionally sabotage critical thinking. You may have seen people use some of these negative strategies before, or maybe you have used them yourself in the past. These are ways people turn away from critical thinking and truthful arguments for falsehood and even manipulation. [17]

Lack Of Respect For Reason

Reasoning is the cornerstone of critical thinking. It is extremely important for forming sound arguments and deriving a conclusion from your premises and arguments. In everyday situations, people cannot accurately use critical thinking skills without a certain level of reasoning. [21]

As man's tool of understanding the world, it is necessary. It is the method of identifying entities through one's senses, integrating your perceptions into concepts, gaining knowledge through integration, integrating that knowledge into the rest of your knowledge, and finally evaluating and manipulating ideas and facts.

You can consider reasoning to be the process of thinking. It is defined by clarity, not gut thinking or intuition, and requires clear and identifiable building blocks. Additionally, reasoning is an organized way of thinking as it is systematic and purposeful. It concentrates on the fundamentals of the argument and uses clear methods of logic and deduction to reach a conclusion. [21]

As a clear way to achieve knowledge and understanding, the ends towards which it is used to end up defining the validity of the method of reasoning. Remember, your conclusion is only as strong as the premises and arguments that back it up.

Knowing the importance of reasoning to sounds thought patterns, it is no wonder that reasoning is so important to critical thinking. But what happens when someone does not have any respect for reason?

Suppose someone is making the argument that a severe storm is not about to take place. However, all logic points to a storm coming within minutes: it's dark, cloudy, the wind is blowing, and thunder and lightning have taken place.

Someone who lacks respect for reason would adamantly disagree. They support their argument by saying the clouds are just passing through and thunder and lightning is not usually a sign of a storm. They continue to claim that a storm will not happen, even though all evidence points to a storm.

Their methods for reasoning quickly fall apart. There is no clarity in their argument. Instead of building an argument from the evidence around them or the concrete facts, they are making the argument based on vague premonitions.

Someone who does not have respect for reasoning refuses to see it in an argument. Because of this, they are not attempting to use critical thinking skills which require a level of reasoning.

Intellectual Arrogance

Intellectual arrogance is when people become full of themselves because of what they know. Sure, that person may be very smart, and that is fine, but when they have a pompous exaggerated view of their ability and knowledge because of their intelligence, which is when it becomes a problem. [5]

There are a few characteristics that signal someone who is intellectually arrogant: [5]

- They know they are the smartest person in the room and make it known that they think their opinions are the only ones that count.
- Most of the time, people will not tell them they are intellectually arrogant, and if they do, then the intellectually arrogant person will not believe them. They have to discover it on their own.
- Their own recognition of their intellectual arrogance can lead to their downfall. Sustained success can give a person a feeling of infallibility or invincibility. Once that is gone, the person can feel lost.

Intellectual humility, however, is the opposite:

- These are the people who are smart enough to recognize that all ideas and opinions have some kind of value and that all issues and problems are multifaceted.

- They possess the ability to work as a group and do not put themselves above others.
- They do not rush to judge others.
- They try to elicit the best from every person they encounter.

A study revealed that a few characteristics that go along with a person who possesses an unhealthy amount of intellectual arrogance and how they are evaluated by others.

For one thing, they do not see themselves as others see them. They see themselves as exceedingly humble and would not dare to call themselves anything close to arrogant. However, other people who know them would think the exact opposite of that. They have seen the arrogance in full force from an outside lens and would definitely say that this person is full of themselves.

Another thing that was found is that in group projects, other team members gave better evaluations to those they felt were humbler. Maybe the intellectually arrogant person contributed a lot to the project, but the way they felt that they were above everyone else in the group and the way they treated others made the rest of the group think little of them and would rather have worked with less arrogant people. [5]

Finally, people can usually agree on who is intellectually arrogant and who is intellectually humble but it takes time. People will evaluate others genuinely based on evidence to support how they feel about them. If they spend only a short amount of time with someone, they do not have much time to truly draw conclusions about that person. Sometimes, people may find it challenging to determine whether someone is humble or just shy, or arrogant or simply very extroverted.

You may have worked with someone who is intellectually arrogant. If not, you might encounter one someday. Imagine working on a group project. The intellectually arrogant one in the group thinks only their answers are right. They don't accept any opinions from the rest of the group. They try to appoint themselves the leader of the whole operation but do not take the suggestions of others on how things should get done. Their arguments are flawed because they do not listen to the reasoning of the other group members.

Therefore, intellectual arrogance completely derails critical thinking. Yes, critical thinkers are smart, but that is not their only characteristic. They are open-minded, unbiased and open to new points of view. All of this takes a certain level of humility and so the intellectually humble person makes for a better critical thinker.

Unwillingness To Listen

This is the person who many people have encountered at least once. The person who does not listen to what you are saying no matter what. They completely ignore your point of view in favor of their own because they do not agree, or they do not care to hear anything other than what they want to believe.

Someone unwilling to listen does not care to listen to reason, even if your argument is much more valid than their own. Their arguments are false and they are fine with that. Either they know their argument is false but they are too comfortable in that position to change it, or they are unaware they are wrong but they have held that point of view for such a long time they do not care to listen to another one.

There are five key characteristics of bad listeners: [5]

- **Interrupting**: This is probably the easiest to point out. Most people interrupt others, but only to a certain extent. With the person unwilling to listen, they interrupt constantly because they do not want to listen to what you have to say. Their own opinions are much more important to them because they feel that only they are correct.

- **Closed-Mindedness**: People who don't want to listen to others are closed-minded people. Their perspective is narrow, and it does not interest them in learning new ideas. Think of their worldview as a circle they are not willing to step outside of or expand.

- **Too Busy**: With someone unwilling to listen, they might give their opinion but when it is time for you to speak your mind, they say they are "too busy" to listen. They either turn their attention to their phone or some other distraction or they may even just leave altogether. If they remain in front of you, you might get an occasional "uh-huh, sure" from them, but in reality, it focuses them on something else because they do not care to listen to what you have to say.

- **Match Back**: This is when you can tell someone something, a serious story or something that happened to you, but the person turns it around into something about themselves instead. They share something that happened to them that may or may not be similar to your own story and then try to give unsolicited advice on how they would have handled the situation. It is a way to make the situation more about them and make it so they don't really have to listen to you.

Listening is an important aspect of critical thinking. On one hand, it allows you to be open to other points of view. On another, you cannot properly evaluate someone's argument if you are not listening closely to what they are saying.

Intellectual Laziness

Intellectual laziness goes hand-in-hand with passive thinking. It is not thinking critically and not attempting to come to conclusions outside of what you were told. With intellectual laziness, people succumb to the social pressure of what other people around them believe and do not form opinions for themselves.

If there is a problem facing them, they go with the obvious answer, whether or not it is correct. It is the answer that stands out and the first thing that catches their mind, so they go with it and do not look into the problem for what is correct. [10]

Suppose the intellectually lazy person normally follows a certain political view. They are extremely adamant about it and do not accept any outside view. Even if the opposite party says something that is, in fact, correct, the intellectually lazy person will not research for themselves to find that this person is correct, but will reject it just because it did not come from their party affiliation.

Another example is a person who has for their whole life believed that global warming is not happening. They adamantly stick to that belief without taking the effort to research impartial sources to find out what is happening with climate change.

What often happens is that intellectually lazy people fall into the mindset that someone else cannot disagree with them. However, they are allowed to say whatever they want and offend, insult and discredit that person for disagreeing with them. Essentially, they have convinced themselves of their own moral and intellectual superiority but are lazy because they refuse to take the time to consider any other point of view.

Lack Of Respect For Evidence

In most cases, if the evidence presented to you supports your argument then naturally you can draw from it a conclusion that makes sense according to the argument. However, sometimes the evidence given to you is not entirely accurate, and this presents a challenge in determining what kind of conclusion you should be making.

This is where critical thinking comes in and why the use of evidence, and the respect of that evidence, is essential to good critical thinking skills. [16]

With evidence, such an important aspect of critical thinking, when a person does not take into account or respect the evidence presented to them and tries to conclude without recognizing any of the evidence in front of them, ultimately their argument and use of critical thinking skills fall apart. [16]

Imagine this scenario. It is Independence Day in the U.S. and fireworks are an essential part of the day. Your dog is afraid of fireworks and your solution to the problem is to not launch fireworks in your yard this year. However, your brother argues that your dog will be fine and do fireworks anyway while ignoring the evidence that shows that your dog is afraid of them.

You point out that your dog doesn't like loud noises in general due to having a previous owner who shot fireworks and guns around them, leaving them afraid of similar loud noises. You also explain that last year you took your dog to a house where they shot fireworks and the dog ran and hid. Even loud noises like sirens make your dog tremble.

Still, your brother does not respect the evidence presented to them about this and insist that their conclusion that fireworks on the 4th of July are necessary.

Based on the evidence you have found, the logical conclusion is that your dog, who you love very much, is afraid of fireworks and you should not shoot them at your house because of this. However, because all of this evidence was ignored and your brother is adamant about sticking with his argument that celebrating the holiday requires fireworks, his argument does not present a logical conclusion in the case of your dog's fear.

False Dichotomy

A false dichotomy is a type of logical fallacy. It is when only two choices are presented to you, although more exist. It can also be thought of as a spectrum of possible choices between two extremes. They are characterized by either "this or that" type of language or by the omission of choices

A false dichotomy involves people just seeing things in black and white terms without a wider perspective. They essentially say that if A is wrong, B must be the truth. This is another way that critical thinking is derailed because this thinking leads to the misinterpretation of pieces of evidence and reasons.

Typically, a dichotomy is a set of mutually exclusive, meaning that the alternatives overlap and mutually exhaustive, meaning there are other options, alternatives. Express with the words "like" or "or," the dichotomy does not imply extremes or that one option is better than the other. An example is: "Either this test is wrong, or the program is wrong."

However, the false dichotomy is not mutually exhaustive or mutually exclusive. They are meant to force your opponent into an extreme position as the false dichotomy makes the claim that there are only two positions that can be taken on the situation.

Think of this example: "I thought you were a good person, but you were not in church today." This statement implies there are only two options; either you are a good person and go to church, or you are not a good person if you don't go to church.

Of course, there are several other options there that can be considered. Suppose you attend church frequently but you had a good reason to miss this one day. Another option would be that you follow another religion where you are not required to attend church, or you simply don't go to church in the first place. Neither of these options carries the implication that you are a bad person either but the false dichotomy leaves only two options to be considered.

A deductive argument, typical of a critical thinker, requires clarity and little room for alternative arguments. By the time we reach a conclusion in a deductive argument, there should be no more questions remaining and no other options that can be considered.

For example, a deductive argument would say, “All men are mortal. Socrates was a man. Therefore, Socrates was mortal.” This argument does not leave any room for alternative conclusions and does not leave any questions. The conclusion is definite and there is no room for ambiguity.

A false dichotomy carries with it an underlying intolerance for ambiguity, but in a different way than a deductive argument. The false dichotomy carries with it that one answer or the other must be true, whether either is true or not and is usually put forward intending to manipulate the argument in favor of the person making the argument. There is not much reasoning behind this as the deductive argument. Instead, there is an agenda behind it to reach the conclusion that the arguer wants.

Another example of a false dichotomy is, “If you want better schools, raise taxes. If you don’t want your taxes raised, then you can’t have better schools.”

This situation implies there are only two solutions to the problem, higher taxes or bad schools. The intention behind it is clear, it makes it sound like if you do not pick the option of raising taxes then you do not want better schools and this makes you a bad person.

There are several other solutions that go along with improving schools such as a change in school leadership, better use of resources and hiring better teachers. But a false dichotomy comes with a certain intention or an inherent bias towards one option and if you do not choose a certain option between the two extremes presented, then that makes you a bad person.

A common example of a false dichotomy is the saying, “You’re either with me or against me.” Again, this puts the person in front of you in a precarious situation where they are faced with deciding between two extremes. Certainly, they care for you and want to be on your side, but if they disagree with you or if they choose not to be with you on this topic, that implies they do not care about you as much as they do.

Inherited Opinion

Have you ever found that you believe something because your parents told you that as a child and seeing them act it out or talk about it all time reinforced the belief in you? Or maybe you learned something from a friend or a teacher and for most of your life, you believed it. Finally, you either took the time to research it for yourself and found that what you were told was completely untrue.

These opinions you have inherited often fall into the category of political opinions or religious opinions, things your parents probably followed so naturally, you fell into this way of thinking as well. In other cases, they can be scientific facts, beliefs about the world around you or beliefs about people different from you.

Inherited opinion is essentially believing something because someone else told you so. This is another factor that will sabotage critical thinking because it does not involve forming your own opinion based on your own knowledge, experience, and reasoning. It is a form of passive thinking. Someone told you it was true, so you do not take it upon yourself to discover otherwise. [8]

Most of the time, inherited opinions are influenced by social factors. Studies have found that in a lot of cases, certain social beliefs and long-held attitudes are largely the product of the social environment that a person grows up in. [8]

Things like knowledge of foreign affairs and political opinions are highly heritable actions and direct our choices for the kind of social niche's we participate in such as who we spend our time with and the activities that we partake in. [7]

Environmental factors and a person's individual experiences are strong determinants of a person's opinions and beliefs but there is little evidence to show there is necessarily a genetic component that contributes to certain attitudes. These tend to come from a person's personality and the way they grew up. [8]

As an example of inherited opinion, say you live in a small town in a rural part of the country. You were told for your entire life that the big city is bad. The people there are bad, they make poor choices and their values and lifestyle is wrong. Additionally, you were told the city itself is dirty and dangerous because of the crime that runs rampant there. Because of this, you grew up with the mindset that big cities are undesirable and you want to stay away.

However, one day you are in the library and you see a picture of New York City. The landmarks look really cool and the city itself actually seems quite beautiful. As she is passing by, the librarian tells you that she is from New York City and she misses it and wants to go back. From there you find yourself wondering if what you were told about big cities was true.

Finally, you decide to find out for yourself. Despite the protests of your parents and the adults around you, you book a flight to New York. Once you get there, you are amazed. The city is even more beautiful in person. Although crowded and busy, you don't find it to be dangerous and dirty the way you were told. The people you meet are also very kind and helpful.

From there, you change your opinion of big cities. You realize that the opinion you inherited from your parents was wrong and that the city is not as bad as they made it out to be.

Because you took it upon yourself to find out more about a big city, it had changed completely the opinion that you inherited. But what about someone who does not take it upon themselves to find out more beyond they originally told what them?

They don't go out of the way to learn more and broaden

their perspective while eliminating their biases, all traits necessary for a critical thinker. They do not go out of their way to see what other people feel about a certain topic. Those with inherited opinions could find themselves with incorrect opinions on different beliefs, political, religious and more, and they end up with unnecessary biases against different ethnicities and worldviews. They remain trapped inside their own circle without trying to broaden their horizons.

Because of this, inherited opinions will sabotage critical thinking if the person with that opinion is a passive thinker and remains complacent in that form of thought.

Luckily there are a few ways to avoid inherited opinions.

- **Evaluate Biases**: We know that bias completely ruins all critical thinking. You cannot form an objective opinion if you have some kind of bias in whatever situation you are trying to form an argument for. With inherited opinions, more than likely you become biased due to the information you were told. As things you were told and believed your whole life, it can be hard to pinpoint exactly what these biases are. Think of particular topics that people have varied opinions on or topics that are controversial. Are there political, religious or scientific opinions like climate change that you hold because someone around you holds the same opinion? Or maybe it can be something even simpler like what shows you like or what singers you think are good.

Thinking of your own biases is important, but it will also help to think of the biases that the people around you have. Does your grandparent make inappropriate comments about other people? Maybe your father is an adamant believer of conspiracy theories such as the Flat Earth Theory. Evaluate the biases of others to determine whether this is something you have picked up on.

- **Fact Check**: Now that you are aware of the biases that you and those around you have, fact-check them. Do your own research. Read books on the topic, research the history of it, and look at the news reports from a variety of sources to see various points of view. Speak to others who have a different opinion than yours. Join groups, whether in person or online, where people share different opinions on things.

  Now that you have fact-checked these opinions, start forming your own opinion on them. Follow the steps of critical thinking and draw your own conclusions on these topics. Maybe you find that your opinion on the topic remains the same after doing your own research and reasoning. This is fine, there is no requirement that your viewpoint has to drastically change. However, at least now you have formed your opinion on it based on your own thought patterns instead of following others.

- **Tell Others**: Although you have changed your view on various topics based on facts and research, those around you have not. It's difficult to change the opinions of your parents, grandparents or whoever you inherited your original opinion from, but it can't hurt to present facts and try, especially if they hold beliefs that are racist or just flat out wrong.

  In addition to trying to inform the people who you inherited your opinion from, it would also be beneficial to tell others who are inheriting the same opinion, such as siblings or friends. Show them the research you have compiled and tell them your critical thinking skills you applied to come to your own conclusion. Not only are you forming an opinion on your own, but you would also break the cycle for others.

Process Of Critical Thinking

Like any thought strategy, there is a process that goes along with critical thinking. However, what you want to keep in mind about the critical thinking process is that although there are steps that go along with it, critical thinking is not necessarily a "technique". Rather, it is a state of mind.

A true critical thinker says to themselves, "I don't want to believe, I want to know." Critical thinking is intentional, it is specific and the mental state the critical thinker is in is one that drives them to discover concrete information they can utilize in a practical sense. [6]

Critical thinking is the process of thinking about your thinking, while you're thinking, in order to make your thinking even better than it was before. There are two things crucial to the process of critical thinking and the state of mind that it entails.

One of them is that critical thinking is not just thinking, but a means for self-improvement. Not only does critical thinking entail a specific way of improving your thinking, but it also requires skills such as the constant learning and broadening your perspective on life which benefits you in other areas of your life. [6]

Another thing is that the self-improvement that you gain from critical thinking comes from skill in using the standards by which you would appropriately assess your thinking. In other words, it is self-improvement in terms of your thinking through standards that assess your thinking.

Another reason that critical thinking involves such a specific state of mind is that it involves putting certain restraints on your thinking through intellectual standards. So, in order to raise the standard of thinking to a higher level, you are essentially using a method of thinking that is not familiar to you, such as a spontaneous thought or gut thinking where you're just going along with the first thing that comes to your mind. It's about making your brain work harder to raise your standards and improve your thought patterns altogether.

There are a set of basic steps that make up the critical thinking process and the more you use them, the sharper your critical thinking skills will be. These steps are:

- **Reconstructing the Situation**: This involves breaking the situation down to its most basic form. Put it in the simplest words you can understand it in. Break down the argument into its basic premises and conclusion. Determine how they fit together. Ask questions about the evidence.

- **Revealing Hidden Issues**: These would include bias and manipulation. Does the person making the argument fall into any of the traps that sabotage critical thinking such as inherited opinions or intellectual arrogance? Or do they use certain fallacies like false dichotomy? Also, determine what the intention behind making this argument is. Are they genuinely trying to inform or are they trying to manipulate the situation so they come out on top?

- **Making the Best Decision**: This is where you draw your conclusion to the situation. At this stage, keep in mind that rather than choosing an answer because it feels right, you should subject all options to scrutiny and skepticism. Passive thinkers choose the first answer that they think sounds right. Critical thinkers take all the possibilities because the conclusion that seems the most correct could end up being very wrong upon further examination.

Critical thinking is best described as a set of different skills that has some core skills, like applying skepticism, but also has a variety of other skills that vary between individuals.

One of those skills is communication. There are two types of communication that people engage in. One of them is just surface-level communication or trivial communication. This communication doesn't really require any kind of education or any real in-depth thinking. Think of it as small talk or gossip, things that don't really utilize any skills to do it well. This kind of communication isn't all that deep. [6]

The other communication is the type that results in a deep, in-depth conversation. It involves the four modalities of reading, writing, speaking and listening. Sometimes they can be used all together, or sometimes they can be used separately, but all of them require some higher level of thinking and effort. These four things involve problem-solving and critical thinking skills throughout the entire process.

You can think of communication as a transaction between two logics. For example, in reading there is the logic of the author and the logic of the reader. The reader reconstructs the logic of the author into their own experience and they evaluate it on their own. There is a similar process for writing, speaking and listening.

Another skill important to critical thinking is collaborative learning. Collaborative learning becomes useful when it is grounded in disciplined critical thinking. How many times have you been in a group setting where you had to work on a project or solve a problem together but people weren't taking it seriously and group members were displaying actions that sabotage critical thinking such as intellectual arrogance and not listening. Surely not much got done on the project, or when the project was finally completed, it was not very good. [6]

But if you are in a situation where everyone works hard together, everyone puts forward the effort to follow the steps of critical thinking and puts together conclusions and arguments that are sound, valid, and grounded in reason, the result is very different.

Without critical thinking, collaborative learning turns into collaborative mis-learning. It's just a collection of bad thinking thrown together in a messy way that does not yield any positive results and the bad thinking becomes validated among the group.

Some examples of collaborative learning are prejudices, stereotypes, and mass hysteria. They stem from a group of people engaged in bad thinking practices and they validate them amongst themselves.

However, when disciplined critical thinking is present in a collaborative learning-setting, you get a mode of collaboration which is grounded in education, knowledge, and insight.

Curiosity goes hand-in-hand with critical thinking. In

order for curiosity to flourish, there must evolve from disciplined inquiry and reflection. Left to itself, your curiosity will wander aimlessly, leading you into unhelpful, and at worst dangerous, situations. [6]

Intellectual curiosity is different. Here you are still allowing your mind to wander but in a controlled way. It involves intellectual humility, intellectual courage, intellectual integrity, intellectual perseverance, and faith in reason. Intellectual curiosity proves its value because it leads to knowledge, understanding, and insight it can also help to broaden, deepen, and sharpen our minds, making us better, more humane, and more richly endowed people.

You have to be more than curious to reach these means though. You have to be willing to work, willing to suffer through confusion and frustration, willing to face limitations and overcome obstacles, be open to the views of others, and be willing to entertain ideas that many people find threatening.

One final skill that goes along with critical thinking is self-esteem. You might think self-esteem is not very important to your thinking process, but it plays a big role. Healthy self-esteem comes from a justified sense of self-worth and self-worth comes from your level of perceived competence, ability, and genuine success. [6]

However, there is a healthy self-esteem useful to critical thinking skills, and there is an unhealthy version. If a person feels good about themselves for no particular reason other than they are full of themselves that misplaced sense of self-worth clouds their judgment and they fall into the trap of intellectual arrogance.

But if you just have a good sense of self and feel good about the person you are, you will find yourself more confident in your ability to reason in a sound way and will find yourself more likely to think your conclusion is justified after following all the steps of critical thinking.

It is the variety of skills between individuals that explains the need for peer review, between different individuals. One person might be good at timing logic but another person may be good at mathematical logic and another person good at data assessment and so on.

Formulate Your Question

The critical thinking process is essential for solving problems. The process that goes along with it is most often used with ill-defined problems; those that are complex and do not have an obvious answer or an expected solution. Although there is no correct answer to the problems, using the process of critical thinking you can come to a solution that is reasonable and valid.

These types of problems are the kind that requires a systematic approach, one that critical thinking is perfect for. Without this systematic approach, it will be more difficult or even impossible to reach a satisfactory conclusion that makes sense. So, to achieve the best results for whatever solution you are trying to find, you must follow the steps in the critical thinking process in order and carry them out thoroughly as all the steps are necessary to reach a sound conclusion. [31]

The first step in the critical thinking process is to formulate your question. This will help you to clarify the problem at hand.

To take a situation as an example, imagine you have decided you want to live a healthier lifestyle and as part of that you want to join a gym. There are two gyms close to you. You want to choose from and both come with their own pros and cons.

So, the question that is posed to you before you is, which gym should you choose?

One of the most important parts of this step is knowing what you are looking for and explaining it in detail to formulate a detailed question. Layout a list of criteria for you to make your decision. In this case of choosing between two different gyms to join, some things you might look for are the distance from home, how big it is, the amenities they offer and how friendly the people are.

Knowing what you are looking for in solving a problem through critical thinking is an essential first step. A detailed question will guide you as you move forward in the process.[31]

Gather Your Information

The next step in solving a problem through critical thinking is to gather all of your information. Information gathering helps you to weigh out the different options presented to you, moving closer to a decision that hits your goal.

Gather as many details you can about the situation. These include the pros and cons, practical information, and questions you have about the situation. Explore any judgments, arguments, opinions, and conclusions that you can find about the issue, whether this is looking online, reading it in a book, or speaking directly with others. Ask yourself what evidence you can find about this that backup, or even disprove, your experience, beliefs or opinions on the topic. [31]

Think of this phase as going through analysis and interpretation of the information you have gathered.

Also, at this step, you should be able to clarify the problem or situation and ensure you clearly understand the issue you are trying to find a critical solution for. Ask the five W's and H questions (who, what, when, where, why and how) to refine your thoughts on the issue. Some of these might include what is happening, who is involved, what are the stakes in the process and what is the best way to characterize, categorize or classify this?

To be even more thorough, go into a deeper analysis of the matter at hand. Consider other perspectives, beliefs, assumptions, and opinions apart from your own. Do this with an open mind so you can consider as many options as possible. You should also analyze all the facts and any metrics available to corroborate the evidence.

Some questions you can ask yourself are what are you claiming, why do you think, what are the arguments (pros and cons), what assumptions must we make to accept that conclusion, what is your basis for saying that, what are the underlying or hidden issues, and what would success look like to all the people involved in the problem? [31]

Going into the example of trying to find a gym to join, find answers to the details you considered when formulating your question.

You find that Gym 1 is a few miles closer to your house which would give you a more convenient commute. While Gym 1 is closer, Gym 2 has more amenities such as a few group exercise studios, a spinning studio, a pool, and a sauna. Naturally, Gym 2 is more expensive, but it offers more. However, Gym 1 has a robust schedule of group exercise classes you are very interested in.

As part of gathering information, look at some pictures and reviews online, talk to people who attend the gym, and even ask for a tour.

Be as thorough as possible about gathering information because it will inform your answers in the next step.

Apply The Information

This is the stage when all the information you found on the topic comes together. At the formulating a question phase and the gathering information stage, you can consider the "Presentation of the Problem" part of solving a problem through critical thinking. Now, to apply the information phase, we can consider this the "Taking Action" phase of the process.

This is where you consider your reasoning and formulate a conclusion to the situation. Additionally, you will try to evaluate the validity of your argument and solution.

At this phase, this is where you identify and secure the elements needed to draw a reasonable conclusion. Here, you will compile all the data, statements, principles, evidence, beliefs, and opinions from the previous phases and brainstorm ideas. At this point, you will identify possible conclusions and determine the viability of the conclusion you come up with. [31]

At this phase, there are going to be critical questions you will want to ask yourself before coming to a definite conclusion on the issue.

Some of these are what conclusions can we draw given what I know, what can I rule out, what does this evidence imply, what additional information do I need to resolve this question, what are the consequences of doing things that way, what are some alternatives I haven't yet explored, and are there any undesirable consequences that I can and should foresee?[31]

At this phase in selecting a gym example, here you want to put together all the information you have gathered so far and come to a solution on it. Consider what would ultimately be best for you in this situation. Is distance a bigger concern for you or is it the expense? Would you rather be at a gym with a greater selection of group exercise classes, or do you want other types of amenities? Also, consider the other information you gathered such as the reviews and speaking to others.

Consider The Implications

In the last step you have come up with a solution to the problem at hand, but it is not enough to just settle on the first conclusion you come up with. Critical thinking in problem-solving goes way beyond that.

At this phase, it is time to consider the long-term effects of your decision. Perhaps right now it seems right, but what consequences will it have in years to come? This is the thing you want to think about before you settle with your decision permanently.

This is all about assessing the credibility of the solution you came up within the application of the information phase. Here, you want to review any new evidence and ideas generated since you came up with your solution. Evaluate with fresh eyes the validity of the possible solution and probe for weaknesses in your thinking and logic. [31]

At this phase, some questions you can ask yourself are how credible is the claim, how strong is the arguments, do we have your facts right, how confident can we be in your conclusion given what you now know, what are the consequences of this solution, what would it look like in a year if you implemented this solution?

A strategy you can take to guide the process of considering the implications is to start by recapping the critical thinking process, possible solutions and how you arrived at them. Think of any flaws that could have been present in your reasoning. Was there any bias in making the decision? Did you pass over or leave or any important information? [31]

Finally, use the above questions to evaluate the validity of your argument or solution. If you can answer positively to most or all of the questions, then it is safe to say that the implications will not have any significant negative effects on you.

If you cannot answer positively to most of the questions, then it is time to backtrack and reevaluate your critical thinking process. This could mean that you need to gather more information or more correct information. It could also mean that your question was not refined enough so you should go back to the beginning of the process.

In the case of the gym example, suppose you went with Gym 1. What implications will it have on you in the future? It is closer to home and not as expensive as Gym 2 so it will have a better effect on you financially in the long run. It is not as big as Gym 2, and while this may be fine for now, will you find yourself wanting to be around more people and in bigger group exercise classes in the future?

Explore Other Points Of View

After you have considered the implications of your conclusion, the critical work is still not finished as you want to be completely sure you are making the right choice.

This final phase is a chance for you to take a step out of the situation and look at it as a neutral person. Think of this as a moment to explore other alternatives to what you have come up with and see if you can come up with something better.

This step involves speaking to or reading about others who have a different point of view than you. One of the core aspects of critical thinking is being open-minded and able to explore other perspectives. This is very important for figuring out whether the decision you made is the best one and if there is a better one out there that someone else has come to that might fit you better. You might also determine that you can combine someone else's conclusion with yours to make an even stronger one.

In the case of choosing a gym, suppose you decided the answer to your question is that Gym 1 is the best solution for you and your lifestyle at this point. However, it might still be beneficial to you to revisit Gym 2. Take one more look at the perspective of people that go to that gym and find out what makes them happy there. It can help you to further determine whether Gym 1 would be the best answer for you or not.

You might even consider other workout options such as other gyms that you might not have looked at or alternative fitness areas like community centers, the fitness center at your housing complex or even working out from home.

In many cases, solutions made from critical thinking do not just involve a choice between two answers. You might find that one of the two answers is best for you, but then realize there are several other solutions out there to explore and it might take more digging to truly come to the solution to your problem.

Before coming to your final decision, really take the time to narrow down your decision and ensure that this is truly the best decision you can come to before settling on your solution completely. Take the time to question, confirm, validate, and connect your reasoning to your results.

Ask yourself if you can be more precise on your choice, how good was your methodology and how well did you follow it, how good is your evidence and is there anything that you are we missing before you commit to the decision.

Following this process of critical thinking carefully, it will better equip you to make well-thought-out decisions on complex and ill-defined problems. Although sometimes it can seem like with some problems we face, critical thinking is unnecessary, it is something we use every day in either complex choices or issues that do not seem as complex such as selecting a gym to join.

Can Critical Thinking Be Learned?

At some point in your life, you may have heard about how important critical thinking is. For many people, their first encounter with critical thinking comes in school where a lot of the lessons have to do with critical thinking in some capacity. Some may say it is one of the most valuable skills that we expect students to learn in school. Outside of school, we prize critical thinking skills among employers and academics.

Despite how praised critical thinking skills are, is it something that can be learned? In some ways yes and in some ways no.

What we know so far about critical thinking is that it is more an of frame of mind rather than a process or technique that can be learned and includes cognitive and affective domains of reasoning. Cognition is the set of all mental abilities and processes such as attention, memory, judgment, evaluation, problem-solving, and decision making, and affective domains of reasoning meaning our motivations, perceptions, attitudes, and values. So critical thinking is a set of skills, knowledge, and attitudes rather than a set of cognitive skills all on its own. [26]

Because of this, while critical thinking is an important thing to teach, educators often struggle with teaching critical thinking skills because critical thinking has many aspects difficult to evaluate and not everyone has them. Additionally, a lot of students find themselves challenged by tasks requiring critical thought, despite educators attempting to teach them. For example, students good at learning through memorization will struggle when they are expected to use their own judgment to reach conclusions on their own. [26]

Although outside institutions call on schools to do a better job at teaching critical thinking, it ends up being a lot more difficult than it would seem from the outside. Studies conducted over the last 30 years have shown that numerous students are ill-equipped in their critical thinking skills. [30]

It remains difficult to teach because it is not a skill like riding a bike or solving a math problem that has a very distinct step-by-step process. While we can break critical thinking down into steps, the process of thinking is intertwined with the content of thought, or knowledge base, so if you tell a student to look at an issue from a variety of perspectives, if they are unaware of other perspectives then they can't think of it that way. You can teach about how people ought to think but if they don't have the background knowledge, then they cannot easily implement the advice.

Consider what we can call surface thinking. Anything you hear and read is interpreted considering what you already know about similar subjects. Your background knowledge of any subject allows you to interpret it in the best way that you can and come to your own conclusion. Background knowledge also has the tendency to narrow your perspective on the subject as you dive into it deeper because your mind assumes the new information is related to what you've just been thinking about. [30]

With deep knowledge, you can penetrate that surface thinking to find deeper meaning in what you are hearing or reading which can allow you to expand your critical thinking skills. When someone is more aware of the information presented in an argument or problem, knowledge about how to solve it comes to you much easier.

While already knowing about the subject is important, it is not the only strategy. It is also about the ability to look for information that you do not already know. Knowing when to seek new information will serve to expand your knowledge base for not only the situation at hand but future problems as well. [30]

This can be assisted by making connections between similar problems faced in the past. If you had a problem with weeds growing in your garden that you had solved before and a similar situation appears later, you can refer back to that last issue with the weeds and see if there was anything you did there that can help now. Regulating your thoughts and making connections is called metacognition.

While people cannot necessarily be taught critical thinking, critical thinking skills like the ones explained we can gain through practice. [30]

Although not exactly something that can be taught through basic instruction, there are a few strategies you can perform repeatedly to acquire important critical thinking skills. [19]

Attempt to Understand: In all honesty, critical thinking is a difficult skill and the best way to learn how to do it is through the easiest means and working your way up from there. One of the first things you can do is read or listen intending to understand. A lot of times we read or listen to something/someone with the objective of pleasure. To practice critical thinking, do it with the intent of understanding what exactly it is that you are learning.

Practice: Practice makes perfect, and that is especially true with critical thinking. The best way to strengthen critical thinking skills is through constantly practicing all the while being deliberate and intentional in what you are doing.

Transferring Skills: Although you may know how to solve problems in one area, such as through writing, it does not mean you know how to apply those skills in a different area, such as science.

Gain Practical Knowledge: You can read about a topic as much as you want, but experiencing it for yourself is just as valuable. Having a practical understanding and knowledge of an area can help you think more critically about it. Suppose you are very knowledgeable about art but do not know much beyond the theory of it. It would be helpful to go out and experience it whether that is viewing art exhibitions, seeing artists at work or becoming involved in creating art yourself.

Map Out Arguments: This can be a good way to facilitate critical thinking before you really start getting the hang of it. It can make a high-level concept and abstract concept seem much easier to follow.

Be Aware of Your Beliefs: As we know, beliefs can have an influence over critical thinking and sometimes inhibit critical thinking skills. Often, we seek information that confirms our beliefs rather than confronts different points of view. Know of how your beliefs might influence your critical thinking and try to overcome them to think objectively.

We all need to improve and refine the thinking process, to think more effectively. This includes brainstorming without edits, making mistakes, finding the "easy" solutions, and then assimilating them to grow, improve, learn, and ultimately change your thinking. [19]

Ask questions whenever you discover or discuss new information – remember the who, what, where, when, why, how questions. Exercise your critical thinking skills in everyday life, starting with simple problems and topics, and soon you find that critical thinking comes much more naturally to you.

What Is The Best Time To Learn Critical Thinking?

Learning critical thinking can start at any age. There is no limit on how young or old you have to be to learn critical thinking. Anyone is capable of acquiring and enhancing their critical thinking skills.

However, the ideal time to learn critical thinking is when you are young. Learning science and critical thinking should start early. This way it becomes a habit that children carry with them into their adult life that they improve as they get older.

Children are capable of various learning capacities at different stages in their life. A study conducted by French psychologist Jean Piaget in his theory on the cognitive development of children concluded there are four main stages of cognitive development in the early stages of childhood development.

From birth to age two, children learn about the world through their senses and manipulation of objects. From ages two through seven, they are developing memory and imagination and understanding things symbolically, such as the idea of the past and future. From ages seven through eleven, they become more aware of external events and feelings other than their own. [1]

It is the Formal Operational Stage, which takes place from age eleven and up when children are able to use logic to solve problems, view the world around them and plan for their future. This is also the ideal time to begin ensuring children learn critical thinking skills.

But just because children are capable of starting to practice critical thinking skills at the age of eleven, this does not mean everyone starts out with the same level of skills. This is because, even from a young age, people have different levels of cognitive strengths such as how some people are better at memory than logic and reasoning. [1]

Although people start out with different levels of cognitive strengths, this does not mean cognitive skills are set in stone. There are a couple of different ways to help strengthen cognitive skills in a child.

To improve weak cognitive skills, the first step to take on the road to improvement is first identifying what skills the child is weak in through a cognitive assessment which takes a deep look at how the child performs cognitively and identifies strengths and weaknesses.

After that, one of the ways that weak skills can be strengthened by cognitive training also called brain training. This uses fun and challenging mental exercises to target and improve weak cognitive skills. [1]

One of those important aspects of critical thinking that children are starting to develop is determining the validity or credibility of a source. Determination of whether young children are capable of such differentiation has been cause for debate but researchers have shown that children as young as three and four years old already have some sense of individuals differing in their credibility. [33]

At this age they become aware that people around them are capable of making misleading statements. They come to understand the possibility of deception around their preschool years and although the idea of a fallacy or false dichotomy would be completely lost on them, they understand that appearances and reality can diverge, that people may hold false beliefs and that verbal statements might not reflect actual beliefs.

It is important to start strengthening critical thinking skills as soon as possible because cognitive skills have an impact on whether people are successful or whether they struggle in thinking and learning.

Since the basis of critical thinking is how people think as opposed to what people think, there are a few ways to begin shaping how a child thinks and, therefore, strengthen their critical thinking skills as soon as possible: [34]

- **Ask Open-Ended Questions**: These kinds of questions ensure the child has to really think about the answer before responding. You can ask yes or no questions, but they don't actually call for a very deep response. Instead ask, "why do you feel this way?" or "why do you like this?" These encourage the child to respond creatively without having to worry about giving the right or wrong answer.

- **Categorize and Classify**: Classification requires identification and sorting according to some set of rules which is a good skill for a child to learn. Getting them involved with a classification activity every now and then allows them to discover, understand and apply these skills. Classification activities can be anything from sorting laundry to book titles.

- **Work in Groups**: This allows children to understand the thought processes of their peers and discover multiple ways of approaching a problem. It is good practice for working together with others later in life, setting up arguments and premises, and cultivating open-mindedness.

- **Let Them Make Decisions**: It might be useful to help them consider the pros and cons of a situation at this age, but you can let them make the final decision on their own and help them evaluate the decision later.

It is imperative to get everyone to think rationally from an early age. This would solve the world's problems in a lot of ways. In teaching the skills and characteristics of critical thinking as early as possible, it eliminates much of the possibility for closed-mindedness, bias, and inherited opinions which lead to issues such as racism and intolerance.

Critical Thinking Vs. Overthinking

Imagine finding yourself in a situation at work where you are faced with the problem of how to reach more people with your product. This is a prime example of a critical thinking situation where following the steps of critical thinking will be beneficial from forming the groundwork of creating a question, gathering information, and analyzing that information.

But instead of following through with the critical thinking process, the more you think of the problem at hand, you get anxious. You think about what could happen if you don't figure out how to solve the problem in a timely manner: people will stop buying, you won't be able to reach enough people and your business will eventually have to shut down.

Even when you come up with solutions to the problem, no matter how sound, you question those solutions until you feel like they wouldn't have worked out anyway and the whole process continuously falls apart.

You spend a lot of time on it, but find it harder and harder to come up with solutions.

This is a prime example of overthinking. In a critical thinking situation, you would work through the process in a controlled and organized way. With overthinking, all signs of the organization fall away, anxiety creeps in, and any productivity that you once had are gone.

There is a crucial difference between overthinking and critical thinking. Overthinking has overtones of obsessing about a subject; usually someone else's behavior but often your own. You keep replaying what happened in your head as if you're trying to understand it, but the problem is that you're not trying to understand it. You're judging it and you ask questions designed to show that someone is right and someone else is wrong.

With overthinking, you end up spending a lot more

time thinking about a problem than you should, but that does not mean it is productive thinking. Critical thinking is productive. It gets things done; it solves problems in a timely manner, and it is organized and is free of any biases. Overthinking, however, wastes time and mental energy. [23]

In critical thinking, you are actively looking for a solution to the problem, developing steps you can take to reach the conclusion. There are certain strategies and skills you can employ to reach the desired solution. Because critical thinking involves such careful thought, it helps to decrease stress.

Overthinking, on the other hand, does not use a strategy. It involves ruminating, worrying, and over-analyzing. With overthinking, you will find yourself dwelling on a problem rather than finding a viable solution. Because of this, it increases stress, and the more stressed you feel, the more likely you are to focus on the negative aspects of the situation. This creates an ongoing loop of anxiety and critical thinking becomes lost. [23]

Overthinking isn't productive, it's destructive. It stalls you, prevents you from moving forward. Critical thinking, however, is all about seeking to understand. It involves no judgment. You ask questions designed to elicit useful information. Questions that bring you closer to a deeper understanding. [23]

Studies have shown that focusing on negative events can be the biggest predictor of major mental health problems such as depression and anxiety. Part of the reason overthinking causes so much stress is because you are listening to that inner voice critical of yourself and telling you that you are wrong or inadequate. This leads you to overthink situations. [2]

The next time you overthink instead of critical thinking, there are a few strategies you can try to reel your mind back in. Then you can put forward more of a calm and collected mindset and start putting into process your critical thinking skills. [2]

- **Stand Up to Your Negative Inner Voice**: Your inner negative voice perpetuates your overthinking by making you more anxious as it goes on. To stop your negative inner voice from taking hold of you, first, take note of what that inner voice tells you when it comes up. Then think about where these words are coming from. Does it have to do with a current situation such as work or someone you love? Or did it start from an earlier life event that left you feeling inadequate as an adult? After you understand where it is coming from, you can separate it from your more positive thoughts. Finally, whenever those negative thoughts come back, push it away. You can do this by coming up with a set of phrases that talk back to the inner voice such as, "I can do this" and "I am capable of solving my own problems."

- **Choose Your Thoughts with Mindfulness**: An effective way to stop overthinking, thinking with mindfulness is about learning to control or focus your attention in order to increased calmness and self-awareness. This way, you are better able to understand and have control over your own behavior.

- **Change the Way You See Problems**: Instead of facing problems with stress and ruminating in a negative issue, change the way you see and approach the problems you encounter. Instead of seeing a challenge as something bad, think of it as a positive challenge that you will be stronger for overcoming. Accept that you have a lot of control over your own circumstances by having a positive mindset. Commit to overcoming these challenges to feel powerful and proactive in the face of them.

Conclusion

Critical thinking is essential for analyzing information and coming to clear and sound conclusions to any argument you make or any solution to a problem. It requires a process that includes examining evidence and making your own judgments about whatever it is you are thinking about.

As important as critical thinking is, avoid things such as intellectual arrogance, not listening and being quick to judge or else your whole argument for thinking critically falls apart just as fast as it began.

There are endless situations where critical thinking can be used. Looking back, you were probably in a situation that involved critical thinking without even realizing it. However, it is important to understand that it is how you use your critical thinking skills that determine the effectiveness of it.

Above all, critical thinking is a state of mind that not everyone possesses naturally. Although schools attempt to teach critical thinking, it takes consistent practice to train your brain to think critically at any time.

As with anything, you should strive to be the best thinker that you can be. Better critical thinking skills will enable you to face any situation head-on and solve problems with accuracy and efficiency. No matter where you are, in work, in school, or in everyday life situations, you find that critical thinking is necessary.

Despite the endless techniques and skills that come with critical thinking, the best thing you can do for yourself is practice. Practice every critical thinking strategy, take on all the characteristics of a good thinker and actively monitor yourself to ensure you are avoiding anything and every that serves to ruin good critical thinking.

References

1. “4 Cognitive States For Child Development.” Learning Rx.

2. “Are You Overthinking Everything?” PsychAlive.

3. Ash, Eve. “Five characteristics of bad listeners.” (2017). Smart Company.

4. Bailyn, Evan. “The Value of Active Critical Thinking.” (2012). Early Writings of Evan Bailyn.

5. Baylor University. “People with higher 'intellectual arrogance' get better grades.” (2015). Science Daily.

6. “Critical Thinking: Basic Questions & Answers.” The Foundation For Critical Thinking.

7. Barber, Nigel. “What Behaviors Do We Inherit via Genes?” (2015). Psychology Today.

8. DeAnelis, Tori. "Are beliefs inherited?" (2004). APA.

9. "Deductive and Inductive Arguments." Internet Encyclopedia of Philosophy.

10. Dwyer, Christopher. "5 Barriers to Critical Thinking." (2019). Psychology Today."

11. Gambrill, Peter. "Effective Argumentation: Premises and Conclusions." San José State University.

12. Girard, Patrick. "Good and bad arguments." University of Auckland.

13. "Good and bad arguments." Acrewoods.

14. Hasa. "What are Premises and Conclusions in an Argument." (2016). Pediaa.

15. Haplin, John. “Ampliative Reasoning and Informal Logic.” (2010). The Logic Cafe.

16. Horowitz, Sophie. Sliwa, Paulina. “Respecting all the evidence.” (2015). Springer Science+Business Media Dordrecht.

17. Hurson, Tim. (2007). Think Better: An Innovator's Guide to Productive Thinking.

18. “Is it rational to trust your gut feelings? A Neuroscientist explains.” (2018). The Conversation.

19. Kaminske, Althea Need. “Can We Teach Critical Thinking?” (2019). Learning Scientists.

20. Lau, Joey Y. F. (2011). An Introduction to Critical Thinking and Creativity.

21. Landauer, Jeff. Rowlands, Joseph. “Reason.” (2001). Importance of Philosophy.

22. Moore, B. N., & Parker, R. (1989). Critical thinking: evaluating claims and arguments in everyday life.

23. Morin, Amy. “Problem-Solving Is Helpful. Overthinking Is Harmful. Here’s How to Tell the Difference.” (2019). Thrive Global.

24. Nordquist, Richard. “Premise Definition and Examples in Arguments.” (2019). Thought Co.

25. O’Neil, William J. “Intuitive and Non-Intuitive Thinking.” (1988). How to Make Money in Stocks—A Winning System in Good Times or Bad.

26. Pennetieri, Regina C. “Can Critical Thinking Skills Be Taught?” (2015). Radiology Technology.

27. “Our Concept and Definition of Critical Thinking.” (2019). The Foundation For Critical Thinking.

28. Sieck, Winston. "Critical Thinking in Everyday Life." Thinker Academy.

29. "Some Advice on How to Learn Critical Thinking." (2019). A Research Guide For Students.

30. Willingham, Daniel T. "Critical Thinking: Why Is It So Hard to Teach?" (2007). American Educator.

31. "A Systematic Process For Critical Thinking." University of Florida.

32. Elder, Linda. Paul, Richard. "Critical Thinking Development: A Stage Theory." The Foundation For Critical Thinking.

33. Heyman, Gail D. "Children's Critical Thinking When Learning From Others." (2008). US National Library of Medicine National Institutes of Health.

34. "Think About It: Critical Thinking." Scholastic.

Disclaimer

The information contained in this book and its components, is meant to serve as a comprehensive collection of strategies that the author of this book has done research about. Summaries, strategies, tips and tricks are only recommendations by the author, and reading this book will not guarantee that one's results will exactly mirror the author's results.

The author of this book has made all reasonable efforts to provide current and accurate information for the readers of this book. The author and its associates will not be held liable for any unintentional errors or omissions that may be found.

The material in the book may include information by third parties. Third party materials comprise of opinions expressed by their owners. As such, the author of this book does not assume responsibility or liability for any third party material or opinions.

The publication of third party material does not constitute the author's guarantee of any information, products, services, or opinions contained within third party material. Use of third party material does not guarantee that your results will mirror our results. Publication of such third party material is simply a recommendation and expression of the author's own opinion of that material.

Whether because of the progression of the Internet, or the unforeseen changes in company policy and editorial submission guidelines, what is stated as fact at the time of this writing may become outdated or inapplicable later.

CPSIA information can be obtained
at www.ICGtesting.com
Printed in the USA
BVHW031726160120
569741BV00003B/13